Contents

The Author
Stephen Stokes

Steve served thirty years in London's Metropolitan Police before retirement in 2001. For two decades he specialised as a police dog handler, and later qualified as a National Home Office instructor. As a senior staff member of the Metropolitan Police Dog Training School in Kent, he progressed to become acknowledged as one of the country's leading narcotics and explosives search dog trainers. Since leaving the police service Steve has been commissioned for police/customs dog selection and training by both UK and International Agencies.

Steve established puppy and adult dog training classes in 1990 and has successfully managed the club since. He is now in full-time self-employment as an instructor and behaviourist dog trainer, with a unique style and versatility in training methods. In order to remain current as both an instructor and handler, Steve also works his own dog at major events in the specialist discipline of explosives search.

The Illustrator
Bill Mevin

Bill Mevin studied at Liverpool School of Art before joining Gaumont British Studios as a trainee film animator under the auspices of David Hand (top Disney Director of Snow White and Bambi). David appointed Bill character designer and this led to animation work on the first British full-length cartoon film "Animal Farm" as well as various shorts.

Later he entered the world of children's comics, and for several years drew many well known TV characters including Dr Who, Popeye, Bugs Bunny, Yogi Bear, Bill and Ben, Space Patrol and many more. He then created a cartoon strip satirizing the American television soaps, Dallas and Dynasty, which was bought by the Daily Mail and was given the star treatment under the title "The Soapremes". Latterly Bill drew the world famous cartoon strip "The Perishers" that appeared in a UK national newspaper the Daily Mirror until the series ended in 2006.

Acknowledgements

Due to my busy work schedule and many other commitments, this short guide to puppy training has taken me some time to complete. In finally coming to the end of this exciting project, I just want to acknowledge and put on record my thanks to some special people who have contributed to its completion.

My first thoughts are of my parents, who throughout my life supported and guided me. I vividly remember the day they drove me to Hendon Police College and we said our goodbyes on the edge of the parade square. That was the start of a career in the Metropolitan Police which ultimately enabled me to write this book.

Another person who has been a big influence in my life is Geoff Padgham, a police colleague and close friend for over 40 years. Without his enthusiasm and support, I seriously doubt whether this book would have gone to print. His confidence in my ability as a dog trainer is equally reflected in his desire to see the finished article. With a friend like him I consider myself to be a very lucky man.

My thanks also go to Bill Mevin the multi-talented artist who through his cartoons has perfectly captured the amusing anecdotes of human and puppy behaviour.

For Thinkpad Print & Design for all their help and support with the printing of this book.

Last and by no means least, I must mention all the dogs that I have owned, trained and professionally worked. Their unconditional love and devotion has been inspirational and I consider myself privileged to have shared part of my life with theirs.

Thanks to you all and I hope you like the finished product.

Introduction

By reading this introduction, I must make the assumption that you are either considering buying, or are the proud owner of a puppy. Congratulations and welcome to the wonderful world of dog ownership.

Throughout my childhood I was blessed with kind, loving and caring parents. Having begged and pleaded with them to have a puppy of my own, they eventually agreed and allowed me to take on that responsibility and all it entails. This early experience of growing up together forged a wonderful relationship, the fond memories and feelings of which remain with me today.

Since then I have been extremely privileged to have worked and trained a variety of dogs in a professional and private capacity. I have never felt that it was just a job, but more a hobby and I constantly look forward to my daily challenges. With the correct approach, patience, kindness and a lot of hard work, the end result can be a wonderful experience, which will lead to a unique friendship that no human can match.

I know from personal and professional experience that puppy training can sometimes prove to be a complete nightmare. This practical and simple guide to responsible puppy ownership will make the experience a happy one for you and your dog.

Steve

Section 1
Owner's Commitment to the Puppy

All too sadly a small number of people purchase or acquire a puppy or adult dog with very little thought to the commitment needed and eventual outcome. It saddens me to mention that on a daily basis, a large number of unwanted healthy animals are euthanized. If potential owners devoted sufficient forethought before acquiring a puppy, this tragic trend could be reversed.

With the pressure of today's modern pace of life, our time is very precious. Before proceeding with the purchase of a puppy, serious thought must be given to the long-term commitment of owning a pet. This decision will change your lifestyle, particularly in respect of reducing free time, creating additional expense and developing a unique dog and owner friendship.

In order to be convinced that your decision to purchase a puppy is the right one, it is my intention to challenge you with some difficult questions. Ask yourself the following:

- Have you got sufficient patience and enough free time to commit to your new puppy?
- If you are working full-time, who will feed, exercise and care for the puppy's needs in your absence?
- Does your income allow you to budget for a puppy?
- Are you physically able to cope with your chosen puppy and ultimately the dog's demands?
- Does your home and garden provide adequate space?
- Do you have a family and will they welcome a new addition?

- Are you confident that your existing pets will accept a new puppy in the home?

- If the answer to any of these questions is "No", then perhaps you should reconsider your decision to buy a puppy.

Having posed these challenging questions about puppy ownership, it is only right to attempt to address the key issues for your consideration. Be under no illusion that a decision to purchase a puppy should never be taken lightly. This long-term commitment will require daily feeding, playing, training, exercising and grooming which potentially can last for many years. Puppies can be very demanding and, like children, they need you to guide them along the way and demonstrate the utmost patience. Rarely will a puppy learn something the first time, so you will need to repeat time and time again many of the training techniques and exercises described later in this book.

Without getting into the specific needs of the different breeds of dog, when the moment presents itself, you must take the opportunity to use that moment for training. This could happen hundreds of times a day and cover numerous types of behaviour e.g. toilet training, barking, chewing, recalls, feeding, lead walking; the list is endless. It may only take seconds to praise your puppy for good behaviour, but it is vitally important that your dog knows right from wrong as early as possible. Their attention span can be short so the more you can disguise their training with a perception of playing and fun the better.

The full cost of owning a puppy and ultimately an adult dog, is a vitally important factor to consider. Apart from the initial purchase price you must consider the daily, annual and unexpected costs involved in responsible dog ownership. Food requirements can vary enormously particularly if you consider the extreme difference in size between a great dane and a miniature poodle. Consideration must also be given to the initial equipment you will need to buy, such as leads, collars, bedding, puppy crates, food bowls and grooming tools. Vet's fees for puppy inoculations, annual boosters and unexpected treatments must be budgeted for (Section 6 gives further guidance on this subject).

At the risk of stating the obvious, you must consider whether you as the owner can physically manage a growing puppy and, in the course of time, a fully grown adult dog. It is worth doing some research and meeting other dog owners who can share their experiences of your chosen breed. All puppies look cute and cuddly when they are very young, but in nine months' time you could have a monster of an adult dog that is a real handful.

The size and make up of your home and garden is a key factor in choosing the right type of dog. You may live in a tiny flat which would only lend itself to a smaller breed. Another consideration is the cost of fencing and securing your garden to prevent the puppy escaping. If you share your home with a partner or other family members, their views must be taken into consideration during your selection process. Another consideration is the number and mix of animals that you already own, and whether they will make for a friendly and harmonious living environment. Some damage (chewing, scratching, urinating, etc) in your home and vehicle is a probability. As an owner, you are legally liable for injury or damage caused to other persons or property. Pet Insurance is a must, not only to cover veterinary costs, but also for third party liability. It is not easy to give you all the answers to this complex subject, but you must make a reasoned judgement based on your own personal circumstances.

I make no apologies for attempting to put you off puppy ownership in this section, and have concentrated on highlighting the serious commitment needed to become a responsible dog owner.

Section 2
Breed & Puppy Selection

The selection of a puppy is a very personal matter. Some people continually return to their tried and trusted breed, which has served them well and been a constant companion and friend throughout their years. Others may not have owned a puppy before and select through personal choice or recommendation. Very few dog breeders will try and put you off purchasing one of their puppies, as they need your money to support their business. So, before choosing a puppy it could be helpful if you spent some time at a local dog training club where you would be able to observe the different breeds, their behaviour, learning abilities and their temperaments. It may be possible to speak to the trainers and various dog owners and ask probing questions. A visit to your local veterinary surgery will also be of use, as they know which particular breeds can suffer from different ailments.

If one of your friends is agreeable, you may be able to experiment by looking after their dog over a weekend period. In this way you will experience the highs, lows and commitment needed for responsible dog ownership.

I would strongly advise that you never purchase a puppy from a pet shop. The majority of these animals have been born at puppy farms in despicable conditions, taken from their mothers at an early age and have experienced a 'battery hen' environment. This will result in a sick, unhealthy and often nervous puppy. Do not be tempted to buy a small puppy on

15

looks alone. Although it looks cute at this stage of its life, it may grow up to be completely unsuitable for your home surroundings.

The following guidelines will help you to make the right choice:

- Your first consideration should be the choice of breed – large or small with a long or short coat

- Your second consideration should be your choice of the puppy's sex – male or female

- Your third consideration is either a pedigree or crossbreed

- The Kennel Club can advise on reputable breeders

- You must decide if you want one or more puppies

- The puppy should not be in a kennel environment, but living in a family home and ideally with other pets

- The puppy should have received its first inoculation and worming before collection at eight weeks of age (no older)

To assist in selecting your breed of dog, you should get a pen and paper and make two columns titled: 'For' and 'Against'. When compiling your lists you must be completely honest and ensure you write all considerations down. In this way a pattern will develop which will point to the breed of dog that is best suited to your personal circumstances and preference.

Once a suitable breeder has been selected, it is essential to see the litter of puppies with their mother. If the mother appears nervous and is reluctant to let you approach her puppies, then you should consider another breeder. Visit the litter on different occasions and try to see them both feeding and playing. You will quickly observe which of the puppies is dominant or noisy and which is nervous or shy. If the breeder is unwilling or unable to comply with any of these reasonable requests, my strong recommendation would be to walk away and consider an alternative breeder.

If you have children, on the first occasion you visit a breeder it is best undertaken without them. Children are naturally drawn to the quiet cuddly pup, and once they have held it and felt the warmth of its exploring tongue they are already smitten. By examining the litter yourself you can make a mature reasoned decision, and then later tell your children which puppy is theirs. In this way there is much less chance of family upsets and arguments.

Assuming you go to a breeder wanting to buy only one puppy, don't let your heart rule your head. If you can't make up your mind, don't buy two puppies! If however you must, different sexes are preferable and avoid two brothers or two sisters. From experience, related puppies can develop nervous problems due to pecking order disputes which can lead to fighting. Additionally you have double the work, cost and responsibility. Remember, if you make the right choice you will have many years of fun and friendship. However, if you make the wrong choice, you will have many years to regret it.

Section 3
Puppy Collection & the First 24 Hours at Home

This section of the book will cover the key practical tips to help you through the first 24-hour period with your new puppy. There will be a number of burning training issues that will become apparent, and quite rightly deserve a fuller explanation. I deal with these important issues in much greater depth in other sections of the book.

Well, the day has arrived to collect your new puppy! If you are fortunate and don't have too far to travel then collection is easier. However, a long journey might be unavoidable and here are some suggestions that will help:

- Ask the breeder if you can collect the puppy in the morning and request that the dog isn't fed prior to collection. It may help prevent car sickness.

- Don't travel alone. Take a family member or friend to help. Remember this puppy will be alone and away from the comfort of the litter for the first time.

- Take a cardboard box that will be big enough to accommodate the puppy. Cut down one side and remove the top so you can easily comfort and handle him or her inside the box. This makes for a secure environment during the journey and prevents the puppy from sliding around on the seat. If necessary the box can also be adapted to secure it using the vehicle seat belt.

- You will need towels, kitchen roll and baby wipes. If your puppy is sick during the journey, it can be cleaned up quickly and easily without soiling either yourselves or the car interior.

- Before leaving the breeder, attempt to get your puppy to go to the toilet and spend time playing before the journey. With a little luck he or she might sleep all the way home.

- Check that you have all the necessary paperwork. If the puppy has received its first vaccination, your vet will require the medical record. A diet sheet will explain the meal times and amount given. Normally the breeder will give you sufficient food to last a few days.

When you arrive home, immediately take the puppy out into the garden. At first it may just sit by your legs. If you slowly and carefully move away, the puppy will naturally follow you around. Avoid talking and allow the puppy to concentrate on its new environment. By not overtly communicating at this time it will stimulate a natural desire to relieve itself.

Once the puppy has relieved itself, take it into the room you have designated for sleeping and feeding. This is normally the utility room or kitchen. This is a good time to feed your puppy, and the food should be provided in a bowl placed inside a puppy crate with the door left open (see Section 4). Place a bed in the crate and if the puppy wants to sleep, encourage it to use this area. A puppy needs to go to the toilet regularly, so remember, when the puppy wakes up it will need to relieve itself again.

If there are children in your household it is important to control their natural enthusiasm and do not let them rush to pick up the puppy. A number of dogs receive serious injuries as a result of children dropping them. If the puppy is asleep, leave it alone. Discourage visitors for the first couple of days and allow your puppy to settle into its new environment. When playing with your new puppy don't overdo it and be mindful that little and often is preferable.

Just before your bedtime when you hope to get some sleep, take your puppy out into the garden to go to the toilet. Having successfully relieved itself the puppy should ideally then be placed back into the crate to settle down for the night. You could consider leaving either a ticking clock or a radio on in the same room just to help break the silence. When left alone, your puppy may bark or whine for just minutes or even hours. You cannot be sure about this length of time as all puppies are different. I would strongly advise that you do not return to try and comfort your puppy. If you do, this will only confirm to the puppy that if it makes enough noise you will come back into the room. I know that

some people may find this harsh, but by responding to the noise you will be making a fundamental error that will cause you further problems in the future. As the master, better to be firm and kind now, or you will suffer weeks of sleepless nights. **Never** take the puppy upstairs to bed with you. This is a slippery slope that can cause serious problems at a later stage in the dog's development.

The following morning, before you attend to your own needs, go down to the puppy, remove it from the crate and immediately take it out into the garden.

Repeat the process of toilet training when the puppy was first brought home as previously described in this section. It will obviously be pleased to see you and may spend a lot of time playing before going to the toilet. Be patient and get used to standing out there in a dressing gown and holding an umbrella. In the long term, all the effort will be worth it.

Meeting Family & Other Pets at Home

If you have young children and expect them to care for your new pet, then think again! Children have an attention span similar to a puppy, so even with the best intentions they will soon lose interest. It is one thing to have fun playing with the dog, but it is another to have to clean up their potential mess. Children often encourage puppies to chase and play-bite them, so you should only let them interact under your supervision. To avoid situations like this use a baby-gate or a playpen. This allows both child and puppy to have their own space.

If you have other pets at home and introduce a new puppy it could upset the natural balance of their environment. Depending on which animal it is, they will be inquisitive about the new arrival. Control your pets and do not allow them to chase or frighten each other. If it is another dog allow it to smell the puppy but avoid any behaviour that could cause stress to either one. Take things slowly, avoid rushing the issue and try not to be over-protective to the puppy. Make sure that the older dog continues to feel special making as much fuss of him as the new arrival.

Section 4
Puppy's Home Training

Crate Training

The crate is a vital piece of equipment and having reared numerous puppies I would not consider doing so without the use of one. The puppy will have the comfort of knowing that it is a place of refuge, peace, pleasure and will willingly enter it day or night. If you are a first-time puppy owner you may be thinking, why not just use a normal dog bed? The answer is, the crate restricts the movement of your puppy and the importance of this approach is explained in this Section.

Although the initial cost of purchasing a crate can be expensive, the long-term benefits are considerable. Dogs naturally like to sleep and relax in a 'den', and this device will be its substitute. Always make sure that the crate will accommodate your dog when it is fully grown. You do not want the additional expense of having to buy a second and larger crate after just a few months use.

Place the bedding at the far end of the crate and by the exit door leave absorbent paper. A dog will naturally avoid soiling in or near its sleeping quarters, but if has no choice it will choose to relieve itself on the paper.

To encourage your puppy to enter the crate willingly, I would advise that all meals be placed in the cage. Leave the door open and allow the puppy to eat without distractions. To avoid making the crate floor wet, a water bowl can be attached off the floor on the inside of the cage. The absorbent paper placed in the crate to accommodate puppy 'accidents', will then only be wet with urine from the puppy.

The crate should never be used as a punishment cell, but should be closed and secured at night. If the puppy is wearing a collar, ALWAYS remove it when the puppy is left alone in the crate. This is to ensure that no unfortunate accidents occur where the puppy could hook itself onto the crate bars.

The benefits of a crate only become apparent when you see the home damage a young dog can cause in a relatively short time. There are real dangers to a puppy of ingesting harmful substances such as cleaning fluids or biting into electrical wires to fridges, freezers, televisions etc. I have also seen luxury kitchens and hallways destroyed as a result of dogs left to roam unsupervised.

Also consider their use as a secure area when travelling in the car and when taking your puppy on holiday and even visiting friends. Remember this is an extension of their home. The crate will fold down very easily and can be as convenient to carry as a suitcase.

Bedding

From experience of rearing numerous puppies, I would suggest that initially you save your hard earned cash and make do (for a few weeks anyway) with an old blanket or jumper for your puppy's first bedding material. Your precious little dog will not appreciate the Louis Vuitton designer bed that costs a fortune and will almost certainly rip it to pieces.

An advantage of initially using an old blanket or jumper is that your scent will be impregnated into the material. This will reassure the puppy that you are still around albeit that you are probably asleep in your own bed in another room or even on another floor of your home. It is essential that you remove any buttons from your old clothing bedding as these could be hazardous if swallowed. Once your old clothing has completed its initial use, an excellent form of new bedding is a product called 'Vet Bed'. It is quite durable and has a fluffy top layer that you can cut to size. It is machine washable so like your own bed linen, wash it regularly to keep it clean and free from unwanted odours.

Toilet Training

I regularly hear from many dog owners of the problems they have encountered whilst attempting to get their pet clean. One thing is for sure, it takes commitment and patience. There are numerous products on the market that claim instant success but in reality this is simply just not true. Having said that, you can get a puppy clean in a very short period of time and this is how I have managed it:

25

With the correct use of a crate you can have success almost immediately. In the early stages the puppy must be confined to only a few rooms i.e. kitchen, hall, utility room, etc. If at all possible try and prevent using any rooms that are carpeted. Once a puppy has fouled a floor covering like this you will never remove the odour completely and this unwanted behaviour will be repeated no matter how good your cleaning materials are. The dog has been taught to defecate almost at any time and anywhere when it was with the puppy litter. We need to re-train the puppy's thought process and teach it to relieve itself outside in the garden. To successfully achieve this goal you will be required to take your puppy outside at least every hour and sometimes even more frequently. This includes the moment he wakes from a sleep or he has just eaten. Once outside, take him to an area that you would prefer him to use as a 'toilet'. To prevent him from moving around you could use a lead. Avoid talking to him and allow the puppy to sniff the ground as this will stimulate him to relieve himself. At the point the puppy is having a wee or a poo just gently repeat the command 'EMPTY'. Repeat it parrot fashion until he has finished and then praise the puppy enthusiastically.

If you talk to your puppy before he actually starts to go to the toilet and use unnecessary phrases such as; "Be a good boy" and "Don't wee back in the house", he might sit and look at you turning his cute head to one side to stare. At this point he hasn't got the slightest clue what you want him to do but is happy to listen to you and is content that you are with him. As young as this puppy is, he is like a sponge and wants to understand you as quickly as he can. Puppies learn at an alarmingly fast rate and this is why you must get it right at the very beginning. Remember 'FIRST TAUGHT, ALWAYS REMEMBERED'.

After a short period of time, your puppy will understand that 'EMPTY' means go to the toilet, and with time will relieve himself on command. Remove faeces immediately as, apart from being a hygienic thing to do and an offence to leave it in a public place, this will prevent your puppy from developing coprophagia (eating its own mess). Many people have told me that they have used newspaper in the home and trained their puppy to defecate on it. I do not recommend this method. Yes, it can be easier to pick up, but you are now teaching your puppy to use a room as a toilet. The disadvantage of this practice is that when the paper is removed there is a high risk that the puppy will select anything else that might be used as a substitute, i.e. a door mat, mail, washing left on the floor, etc.

If your puppy does have a toilet accident in the home, it is your fault for not noticing the signs, i.e. just woken, just fed, circling and sniffing the floor. If you can, pick him up quickly and get him outside as fast as possible and repeat the process of saying 'EMPTY' followed by enthusiastic praise. Never smack or rub the puppy's nose in its faeces or a soiled toilet area, as it is only doing what is a natural bodily function. Let's be honest you would not do this to a child whom you are potty training so why do it to a dog? Just think of the psychological damage that could be done! Understand your puppy's needs, continue to be patient and this important discipline can be achieved very quickly.

In conclusion to this part of my puppy training guide, some dogs have a greater learning capability than others, and so the time they take to learn this discipline will vary from breed to breed. In the end and with many trips to the garden they will all get the idea and understand the command 'EMPTY'.

Meeting Visitors

Once the word is out that you have a new puppy at home, you are guaranteed friends will express a desire to visit and meet the latest member of the family. This, of course, is wonderful but be prepared to take control of the situation and actively manage visitors calling to best suit the puppy's welfare and development.

In my role as a behaviourist dog trainer I have visited many clients' properties to address serious problems that have developed over a relatively short period of time. When I first enter their home, normally through the front door, the first thing that I am aware of is someone shouting the dog's name and attempting to grab hold of it. The dog thinks this is a great game and avoids the rugby tackles of various members of the family trying to stop him from reaching his prey: you, the visitor. Alternatively some owners choose to lock their dogs away in the 'west wing' of their home to prevent them from hearing anyone arrive and deny contact with all visitors.

A home visitor is a great social event and your dog should be part of the welcoming committee but in a controlled manner appropriate to the circumstances. The following advice will help you welcome visitors properly:

1. When the door bell rings your puppy may bark or show signs of interest so praise him.

2. Put him on the lead and walk him to the closed front door.

3. Call out through the closed front door that you are training your dog and that he is on the lead.

4. Open the door to the ajar position and say hello to your visitor(s). Tell them that when they are invited in, to stand by the door which should then be closed, and to avoid making any eye contact or verbal directions towards the puppy.

5. In order to ensure that the puppy is not too close to the visitor(s) when they are invited in, he should be walked back further away from the front door entrance.

6. The human group should then exchange greetings in the normal way before anyone approaches the puppy.

7. Once this has been completed we can now involve the puppy. Ask a visitor to approach your dog with a pre-prepared food treat in the palm of their hand. This can be either the puppy's regular food or a special treat designed for training purposes.

8. Their hand should be placed down in front of the puppy at floor level. This approach will avoid the strong possibility of the dog jumping up when taking the treat.

9. More than one person can do this and very quickly your puppy will recognise that jumping up at visitors is unacceptable.

10. If the puppy attempts to jump up at the visitor(s) you should be able to control him with the lead.

11. Keep the dog on the lead until the excitement of the visitor's arrival has subsided. The time this takes can vary from dog to dog but when calm you may then be able to let him off the lead.

12. The most difficult thing for you to achieve is to control visitors' actions. Don't allow them to pick the puppy up, and avoid children running around calling to him. If this type of behaviour is allowed, the puppy will of course chase around and ultimately jump all over them. Children react to this with a little panic, then tend to scream and raise their hands resulting in the dog jumping up. This is not what you want to teach your puppy to do when children visit!

13. If, when visitors are present, your dog seems to be getting over-excited, place him back on the lead and calm him down with slow gentle strokes.

Grooming & Daily Examination

Other than enhancing your puppy's good looks, grooming is another way of monitoring the dog's wellbeing. Each breed will require different combs and brushes, etc and choosing the wrong type can cause the puppy unnecessary discomfort. Visit a professional grooming parlour and ask for their advice. They will be only too happy to help. Some breeds will require their services on a regular basis and that early experience is essential. This hands-on approach greatly enhances the bonding process and gives the puppy reassurance that this is a normal procedure.

It is also essential that on a daily basis the puppy is handled to prepare him for future physical examinations and treatments. You should run your hands over his entire body, feeling for any abnormal signs. Check all the orifices and get the puppy comfortable with being handled, especially around his legs, paws, tail, ears, eyes and mouth. Gently open his mouth and run your finger along his gums and teeth. He will start to lose his milk teeth from around sixteen weeks of age and his adult teeth develop from around six months. This regular examination will benefit you both when a visit to the vet at a later stage is required.

Section 5
Avoidance of Puppy Behavioural Problems

Damage

If your puppy is left alone unsupervised, be prepared for some nasty surprises. Apart from the obvious damage that can occur, there is an even greater risk of personal injury. They are inquisitive and will explore any area that is left for them to freely roam. As previously mentioned in Section 4, but is worth repeating, the kitchen area will contain numerous hazards such as cleaning materials, waste bins, electrical points, etc. Make sure that these are secure and that the puppy has no access to them. The crate is the safest place for your puppy when you are not supervising him.

If you see the puppy chewing your best silk rug or ripping the stuffing out of the three-piece suite, it is human nature to lose your temper. The puppy is only doing what he believes is acceptable and will not understand why you are screaming at him and at the same time turning crimson. If they are caught in the act of destruction give a sharp command 'NO', but never lash out or use physical force. Remove them from the situation and engage their brain by playing with a proper toy or take them for a controlled walk. Avoid coating furniture with mustard, Tabasco, lemon juice, etc. Some breeds actually enjoy it and see it as their Saturday night curry. Destructive behaviour is normally caused by boredom or anxiety.

Separation Anxiety

You must train your puppy to cope with time alone as this will be part of his daily routine. Ensure your puppy is mentally tired before leaving him. Short training sessions will very quickly achieve this. PLACE HIM IN THE CRATE and secure it. Leave a suitable chew in there to keep him occupied. Practice leaving the puppy for very short periods (two or three minutes), and then gradually increase the time. When you are going out, avoid looking at the puppy and saying, "Daddy won't be long, just going to the shops". It won't have a clue what you are talking about. Just walk out of the door and on your return make it as non-eventful as when you left. Spend a few seconds sorting out your own requirements, then remove the puppy from the cage and immediately take him into the garden for an 'EMPTY' and play. Reward all good behaviour.

Biting

This is often confused with mouthing. Don't get me wrong these teeth are extremely sharp and can very easily cause injury. Puppies naturally play-fight with their brothers and sisters by grabbing hold of one another using their mouths. If a puppy uses too much pressure the victim will yelp to tell the litter-mate that it hurt. Most puppies will then adjust their bite pressure and continue to play.

If, however the puppy continues to bully and cause discomfort, the mother will step in. So when you and the children are playing with your puppy, it can easily revert to type and treat you like one of its litter-mates. Playing with your puppy is a positive and a fun thing to do, but the games that you play will affect their behaviour in the future. Calm and controlled games are the most effective, for example rolling and hiding a ball. Tug-of-war can foster aggression and create a competitive environment, as can intense physical play. Avoid pointing at your dog to tell him off or wiggling your fingers in front of him as they make a great target.

Never use your hands to physically punish your puppy. A tap on the nose is extremely painful for any dog and if you persist with this cruel behaviour, your dog will become hand shy and cringe when you raise them. If your puppy is mouthing, stop playing immediately and stand up. You can also use a high-pitched OUCH at the same time. To calm him down the lead can be attached to his collar and a short heel work routine imposed. Another way to avoid this unwanted mouthing is to stop stroking the puppy on the top of its head. They tend to see the hand coming and open their mouths awaiting the hand's arrival. Instead, stroke the puppy slowly down its back or between the front legs on the chest. If you try to ignite a 'spark' by stroking the coat vigorously, you will stimulate excitable behaviour which could lead to mouthing.

Toys

In my opinion, this is one of the most important sections in my book. During my professional home visits, I am amazed at the quantity of sub-standard toys that are not only useless but dangerous. Some are far too small, others rip to pieces in seconds and there is always the dreaded 'squeaker' that seems to be brought to you whilst you are on the phone or trying to watch television.

My own dogs have always benefited from playing with toys. They learn many different skills through fun, whether your puppy is a professional or pet dog, the enjoyment received is undeniable.

There is a big difference between a chew and a toy. When the puppy is left in the cage a KONG is a very popular distraction. You can place small amounts of food inside it and your puppy will enjoy trying to extract it with his tongue. They are safe and will not disintegrate. This is for the puppy to chew and is not a toy. The toy is something that you introduce to mentally stimulate the puppy's natural instinct. Make sure that you buy wisely and that the toy purchased is the correct size for your dog.

There is absolutely no point in leaving a toy box on the floor and expect your puppy to entertain himself. The interaction and bonding is at its greatest when you are playing with him. When playing it is worth considering the following:

1. Always initiate the game.

2. Play for short periods.

3. Do not allow the puppy to grab the toy from your hand.

4. Never chase it around the room when it is holding the toy. This will develop a chase game that you will never win and could lead to problems at a later stage when trying to recall the dog.

5.   Never throw sticks for your dog or allow your puppy to play with them. They are responsible for many serious injuries and even deaths.

6.   End the session before the puppy gets tired or over-excited and leave them wanting.

If your puppy has found a toy that you have deliberately hidden as part of his play, he might be reluctant to give it up. Potentially you would have already removed hundreds of items from his mouth which he shouldn't have had, so when you attempt to grab him he is thinking 'oh here it goes again'. Praise him for finding the toy and tickle him by the root of the tail. Make no attempt to take the toy. Your puppy will enjoy the massage and come closer to you. After a few seconds gently slide your hand up to the collar, take hold of the toy and give the command 'LEAVE'. If he is reluctant to let go, do not tug the toy violently, but use another toy or treat as a trade-off.

Food

This is an even bigger minefield than the toy selection process. There are hundreds of companies after your business and choosing the right food for your puppy is extremely important. Breeders will have their own opinion on what to feed your dog, as will specialist pet stores, veterinary surgeries and other dog owners. You will need to take expert advice on this subject because there is a bewildering range of diets out there. Each breed will have its own nutritional requirements and getting it wrong can cause you and the puppy some worrying times.

The choice is so vast that it would be wrong of me to advise on this matter, however the main selections will be:

Dry complete foods

There is a very large range on the market and the quality varies widely. Some of these products will be specially designed for puppies and if your finances allow it, always buy the best you can afford. Sometimes these foods appear more expensive, but you will not need to feed the large amounts that would be necessary with a lower grade product. It is best to avoid changes in the puppy's diet, so if you find a product that works, stick with it.

Semi-moist, pouch and tinned foods

Again products will vary, but try to select a good quality food which is nutritionally complete and does not require you to add additional supplements.

Natural diets and homemade food

Some owners prefer to prepare their own menu for their dog. Although I admire their effort, it is very time consuming, and not easy to get the right nutritional balance. From experience I have met a number of owners who have followed this path and many of their dogs have become fussy eaters. If you get it wrong, the puppy could be seriously nutritionally disadvantaged during this rapid growing period of its life.

Generally people will look at your dog and make a visible assessment of its well being, purely from its physical appearance. These are: shiny coat, energetic and active, clean teeth, firm stools and most of all a contented and happy dog. If he is fed a well-balanced nutritional food, then these observations will be apparent.

Feeding

Age guidelines for meals will depend on your puppy's appetite but are normally as follows: four meals a day until the age of four months and then three meals a day until six months. The puppy can then be fed twice a day for the remainder of its life. Two meals a day are far better for your dog than one huge portion.

Once you have selected a food and the puppy is eating well, avoid changing the diet. This could upset their metabolism and cause sickness and diarrhoea. If you have to change the diet, do it gradually over a period of a few days to a week. Amounts of food will vary and what the manufacturer recommends could be too much or in some cases too little. If any food is left in the bowl, pick it up immediately and reduce the next meal by that amount.

When feeding your puppy, place the bowl down and introduce a little control before he is allowed to eat. Only do this for a couple of seconds. You are enforcing your dominance and reminding the puppy that you are in charge. Leave your puppy in peace while it is eating. Do not stick your fingers in the bowl or try to remove it. This can cause anxiety and food aggression.

If you have more than one dog, be extremely careful at feeding times. The puppy may attempt to examine what the other dog is eating and interfere. This could lead to a serious situation resulting in the puppy being attacked. Feeding him in the cage will avoid this potential danger and allow both animals to relax.

Never feed your dog from the table. This could lead to drooling and attention seeking behaviours such as pawing, barking and begging. Also, avoid feeding your puppy when travelling as this can cause car sickness. Never exercise after feeding as this could lead to a stomach dilation, (also known as bloat or twisted gut). This is a life threatening condition which will require immediate veterinary intervention. To reduce this happening, feed medium to large breeds with a raised bowl which prevents them from swallowing air while they eat.

Treats are a good way to assist with the training, but keep them to a sensible size and make sure that they are not high in sugar or artificial colourings. Avoid chocolate which is poisonous and can cause serious liver damage. A natural organic treat will always be best such as a desiccated liver tablet. Avoid fatty or salty foods.

Section 6
Puppy's Veterinary Needs / Puppy Parties

One thing is certain; during your puppy's lifetime you will definitely require the services of a vet. Initially it may only be for the yearly health check and vaccinations but as your dog matures, you will almost certainly be paying the vet a visit, either through illness or injury.

Personal recommendation of a particular vet is always preferable. As a rule, vets encourage potential and new owners to visit the surgery and discuss their specific needs. This is an excellent way to make personal contact with your chosen professional vet or group practice, and allows you to plan this in a non-stressful situation. You do not want to visit the vet's surgery for the first time, come face to face with a complete stranger and then hand over your ill or injured puppy for treatment.

TRUST ME – I'M A VET

I would advise that the surgery is as close to your home address as possible and operates a 24 hour emergency service. You should avoid travelling long distances with your puppy which could result in the dog becoming unnecessarily stressed and not getting the fast life saving treatment it may need.

A puppy's vaccinations protect against Canine Hepatitis, Leptospirosis, Parvovirus, Distemper and Parainfluenza. Generally the puppy's initial

MEVIN

vaccination programme of injections will consist of two visits to the vet at eight weeks and ten weeks of age. Some puppies will already have received their first vaccination treatment just prior to leaving the breeder. If this is the case it will be recorded on a vaccination card and should be handed over to you, along with any other documentation when purchasing your dog.

When this vaccination procedure is completed I would strongly advise that your puppy is immediately micro chipped. This simple procedure will prevent any future misunderstanding of who the puppy's legal owner is and aid in the dog's return if it goes astray. You also need to consider that a high number of dogs are stolen and transported all over the country for re-sale. It is a very simple task to run a scanner over any dog and the registered owner's details will be identified immediately.

As a general rule, the vet will advise that a puppy should not interact with other dogs until two weeks after the second vaccination injection. However, that does not mean you cannot take them out of your home! If the puppy is imprisoned for weeks, it can result in a nervous and/or anxious dog. You need to get them used to your car and to stand at the end of your path or drive to let them experience the outside world. Short walks along the pavement are fine, but don't allow your puppy to sniff at lampposts and trees. Keep the walks short and, most importantly, fun.

A booster vaccination will be required one year on from the date of the second injection. Worming and flea treatment is essential. Roundworm, tapeworm and lungworm can be treated effectively and your vet will advise accordingly.

I would advise that your puppy receives additional protection against Kennel Cough, which is administered by a spray treatment up one of the dog's nostrils. Apart from the peace of mind of an additional preventative treatment, it is a requirement for most boarding kennels.

When you make that journey to the vet, make sure that you have the correct equipment on the dog. The collar should be of the buckle type that can be made comfortable around the neck. You don't want it to slip off when the dog is being examined, resulting in your dog trying to jump off the table. Try and help the vet by handling the dog yourself. Keep calm and relaxed because if you get stressed your puppy will sense it and could become difficult when being examined. Be firm but loving and caring.

It is vitally important from day one that your puppy should be comfortable with you examining him. Grooming is when you bond with your puppy and gives you the opportunity to check him for any injuries, infections, lumps and bumps. The bond should be sufficiently strong to enable you to touch your dog absolutely anywhere necessary. On a regular basis you need to check between his toes, open his mouth, brush his teeth and clean his ears. If during any examination you notice any unusual discharge or repeated scratching or licking then you must consult your vet. If your dog requires the assistance of a groomer then this should help with other examinations at the vet's surgery.

For many years now I have tried to avoid sitting with my dog in the designated waiting area at a vet's surgery. There are a few reasons for this as follows:

1. A vet's surgery and its associated waiting area is where most animals come when they are ill, injured or in need of some form of treatment. There may be an animal in the

waiting area that has contracted a contagious illness. In its early life your puppy is in the process of building up its natural immunity so the last thing it needs is to take the risk of catching something from a passing sick animal. So best to avoid waiting areas whenever possible.

2.   Your dog could be subjected to unnecessary stress i.e. other dogs barking or sick animals crying out.

3.   There is unlikely to be sufficient room in the waiting area to allow your puppy to avoid unwanted contact with other animals.

A better approach is to let the receptionist know that you have arrived for your appointment, and either wait outside in the car or street until called in. In this way your puppy is on the table receiving treatment before he knows it, and then once finished he's tasting a nice little treat from the vet to make the visit a positive one. Your vet will also encourage you to come into the surgery every now and then to use the weighing scales. It is important that you monitor the weight of your puppy as it will vary significantly as they grow.

It is worth remembering that a professional veterinary surgeon can study for longer than a medical doctor and offers an excellent level of medical and surgical skills. Our dogs don't go onto a waiting list like the National Health Service and more often than not are seen and treated very quickly. The cost of this service is obviously reflected in the final invoice but be aware that some treatment can be very expensive. I would suggest that you take out pet insurance, or as a minimum put a little amount of money aside in a savings account each month to cover treatment as necessary.

Hopefully you will be the proud owner of a healthy dog that will only require the annual check and vaccinations visit to the vet. In following these few tips I hope your visits to the vet will become a little easier for both you and your puppy.

Puppy Parties

A number of veterinary surgeries offer the facility of 'puppy parties'. Although in principle it is essential that your puppy socialises and meets other dogs, there are a few things that you must take into account before attending any organised puppy party. You need to establish whether the person running these events is qualified to do so and how many dogs are going to be there. The age of the dogs attending is a very important aspect to consider because you don't want your very young puppy to meet much older or

dominant dogs. If this situation did occur your puppy could be chased around and under chairs with attempts being made to lie on top of him essentially exposing your dog to bullying. The size of the room is important as if it is too small your puppy may not have the space to avoid such situations and this in turn could result in stress.

A puppy party is most likely to be the first time that your puppy will meet other dogs and breeds, and you don't want it to be an unpleasant experience. My advice would be to visit the vets and ask if you can watch a meeting first, in the same way that you would for a young child starting at a nursery. If the staff are professionally competent and the environment is friendly and calm, then the experience will be a positive one for your puppy and can only enhance its natural development.

Section 7
Structured Puppy Training (Commands)

Before detailing the most commonly used puppy commands, it is important to have a basic understanding of your pet's behavioural pattern. A dog is a pack animal and without wishing to state the obvious, it thinks like a dog, not like a human being. It quickly needs to learn its place in your pack situation i.e. the family, and the dog should regard you as the pack leader and not the other way around. With basic commands, this discipline can be quickly achieved and leads to an excellent relationship between dog and owner.

No matter how much you are tempted, never strike your puppy. It will lose its trust in you and it will seriously affect its confidence. This concern will make your puppy reluctant to obey and fear the use of your hands. In some cases it could also result in you being bitten in self defence.

Structured training sessions should be kept short. Like a child, a puppy cannot concentrate for long periods of time. As the puppy gets older, sessions can be lengthened and become more demanding.

Remember that a well-trained dog is a joy to own and a credit to its owners. An undisciplined dog is a nuisance at home, and can be both troublesome and dangerous in a public place. The following commands and guidance will help the puppy to become a welcome member of your family and society.

EMPTY

This command is used when the puppy is going to the toilet (See Section 4).

NO

This is a negative command that must be followed with a positive one. When the dog hears the word NO you have a very short time before he continues in the behaviour that you are trying to stop. Your voice and tone should sound sharp and urgent. When you say NO to your dog he should stop momentarily and give you eye contact. Immediately give him a positive command i.e. COME, HEEL, SIT, etc. and be quick to praise when he obeys.

LEAVE

Use this command when you want your puppy to release anything in its mouth. It is very important that they understand the principle of giving up objects. Some may be toys but others could be hazardous. If it is a toy, praise the dog for releasing it, and then allow the dog to have it back. Avoid your puppy from grabbing the toy from your hand. This mugging action could result in you or a member of the family being accidentally bitten. Either way it hurts.

COME

One of the most enjoyable things about owning a puppy is taking it for a walk. This, combined with the confidence that you can let it off the lead in an open space, knowing that you can call it back at any time and that it will respond correctly.

Training for this starts in a confined space in the home. Wait until the puppy is a short distance from you, and then kneel on the floor at its level. Call the puppy's name followed by the COME command.

When the puppy gets to you, give it lots of praise. Try and do this exercise when there are no other distractions. When your puppy has learnt to respond to the COME command, you can progress the training to more open spaces like the garden followed by the park. Never let your puppy ignore a COME command.

If the word COME is said in a dull monotone voice, the puppy will think you are angry (or boring) and will assume that on its return it will be told off. Therefore, it will wrongly learn not to come back when called. If however, the tone of your voice is high pitched and light hearted, the puppy will be eager to return to you expecting plenty of praise and fun. This reward will be enough to encourage your dog to leave other distractions (like people, other animals etc), knowing that you are more exciting than anything else. Take advantage of your dog's initial insecurity. If it is reluctant to recall, run in the opposite direction or hide behind a tree. Your pup will soon come bounding back (pack instinct). Never run after the dog, as in the puppy's eyes this approach is a great game that you will never win. Avoid just shouting his name and not giving the recall command. All you are doing is announcing your location and your dog will see no reason to return. Imagine someone screaming your name continually and not telling you what they want.

Praise is vitally important to continually encourage your puppy to return to you when called. Do Not instantly put the lead on and finish the walk, even if it has taken a long time to get your puppy back. This action will signal that returning to you means the end of the walk and any fun. It will also create problems in the future, as your puppy will also associate the COME command with going home. Grit your teeth and practice, and if need be, return to basic training by putting your puppy back on its lead.

SIT

With the assistance of a toy or treat this exercise is very easily achieved. Allow your puppy to realise that you are holding either one. Raise your hand in front of the puppy's face and the dog will naturally roll back onto his hind legs. Give the command SIT and as he does so reward him with a toy or treat.

If he is on the lead he should be standing on your left. Hold the lead and treat in your right hand and position it above the puppy's head. He will be looking up at you at this point. With your other hand, gently place it by the root of the tail and apply gentle pressure. At this point give the SIT command and reward your puppy. When the dog is in this position calmly praise and repeat the command. Avoid patting or vigorous strokes as this will only cause your dog to get excited and get out of the sit position.

When first teaching this command, practice it for only for a few seconds at a time. When you release your puppy from the sit position remember to give it lots of praise. Gradually lengthen the amount of time your puppy is left sitting, but never let it move until you tell it to do so.

HEEL

Once again the market is flooded with equipment promising you instant success when teaching your dog to walk to heel. From experience, I would suggest a normal collar with a buckle connection, and a leather lead. Get the puppy comfortable wearing the collar most of the time (not at night in the crate). When you are about to feed him attach the lead and walk him to the food bowl. By doing this at an early age the puppy recognises the lead as a pleasant and rewarding experience.

The object of this training is to require the puppy to walk readily and happily on your left side with his right shoulder close to your left knee. The lead should be held in a loop in the right hand, and when the dog is correctly at the heel position, the lead should be slack. Before you go anywhere you must inform the dog that you are about to move. The sequence is: dog's name (to get his attention), command HEEL and then step off with your left foot. To assist with this you can use a treat or toy in your left hand to encourage movement. I use the command HEEL but there are others. Avoid saying "COME ON", as this will be confused with the recall command.

When you are moving forward encourage the puppy with plenty of praise. Try to walk in straight lines. This will be a great help and will avoid your puppy from being stepped on or you falling over him. A football or rugby pitch with white lines is a good way to ensure that you are walking straight. Try and keep your pace at a constant level. If you slow down or speed up, it makes it practically impossible for your puppy to stay in the correct position.

THE TRICK IS TO GET ENOUGH SLACK TO BE ABLE TO FLICK

MEVIN

If your dog attempts to pull, you will hear their breathing become noisier. Most breeds will accept this minor discomfort and tug away in their excited state to reach the park or woods as quickly as possible. This can be dangerous for bull breeds and could result in them passing out as a result of a lack of oxygen. To prevent the pulling you will need to slacken the lead momentarily and 'flick' it. The puppy will receive a quick jolt and as he does give the command HEEL. For an even greater response turn clockwise (180 degrees) and walk back in the direction that you came from. You will only have to do this a couple of times and the dog will soon learn that a slack lead is better for everyone. When doing the 'flick', at no time should the dog come off the ground or slide across the floor. If the dog is pulling, you are strangling it and are totally at fault.

If you exercise the 'flick' correctly the dogs ears will angle back and you may see him licking his lips. The feeling for him is the equivalent of a sudden shock. Immediately encourage your dog to heel and praise him accordingly.

NOTE: WHEN FIRST INTRODUCED, THIS TECHNIQUE SHOULD BE SUPERVISED BY A PROFESSIONAL DOG TRAINER.

OFF

This command should be used to prevent the dog from jumping up. This includes people, work surfaces and furniture. When the dog attempts to jump up, avoid using the DOWN command. This is for a completely different exercise as outlined in the next point and will only confuse him.

DOWN

This control exercise is extremely important. It emphasises that you are the dominant pack leader. This is a submissive position for the puppy and must be taught from an early age. You have a choice of how to teach this exercise. Some dogs are not food orientated and will need a gentle physical approach. To do this place your puppy in the sit position and kneel down on its right side. Place the palm of your left hand at the lower end of the puppies back by the root of the tail and prevent him from moving out of the sit position. Then place your right forearm and hand behind the puppy's front legs and gently slide them away. Do not grab the legs or pull them. As he slides down give the command DOWN in a calm and assertive voice. Once this position has been achieved, make sure that the dog's hips are rolled over making him more comfortable. When the puppy is in the down position avoid using his name or praising him. This will just excite the dog and he will attempt to get up. Just repeat the command DOWN and slowly stroke along his back. If he attempts to get up, place a little pressure on his shoulders and repeat the command. Do not get agitated or shout. Keep calm but assertive.

Keep the dog in this position for a short while and lengthen the time as the puppy becomes more confident. To release your puppy from the down, swivel yourself in front of your dog then say his name and give the SIT command. To encourage a quicker movement you could clap your hands together as you say the word 'SIT'. Do not allow your dog to get up from the down position unless you authorise it.

The other method is to use a food treat. As before, have the puppy sitting and then lower a treat down between his front legs close to his chest. Keep your left hand in the position as described above. When the puppy is down, give the command DOWN. Hold the treat in your fingers and allow the dog to nibble or lick it. Keep repeating the command making sure that the dog is comfortable. If you give the treat up too quickly your puppy will attempt to get up.

As the training progresses, you should be able to stand up and use voice commands to get your puppy in the down position. Never call the dog to you from the down position, always place them in the sit position first. This should be followed by praise before releasing your puppy from the SIT command.

Section 8
Puppy Walking

Puppy Training Classes

Other than the limited time your dog has spent at puppy parties, a decision will have to be made about his attendance at professional training classes. Naturally there are mixed views and even stronger opinions as to how to proceed with this. Your decision on which way your puppy should be trained will have a huge impact on the outcome of your dog's personality and his acceptance within the community. Whatever you do, you must avoid rushing to the nearest club and signing up without doing your homework. A personal recommendation is always preferable. Visit different clubs and observe their techniques and how they interact, not only with the puppies, but with the handlers and their families. When you walk in for the first time you should be made to feel welcome, regardless of what breed of dog you have purchased. Don't be pressured into signing up for a course as soon as you arrive. Explain that you are visiting a number of clubs and would like to sit and watch a lesson. If this explanation is greeted with indifference or excuses as to why it's not convenient, then try somewhere else.

You should experience a welcoming chemistry with the instructor that gives you confidence in his or her ability. Their qualifications and experience are paramount and can easily be verified. Normally classes will run over a six week period with each lesson lasting for about one hour. Ideally there should be one instructor who will be responsible for the complete training package. Under no circumstances send your dog off to a 'boot camp', where it will be returned after approximately two weeks allegedly fully trained. This boarding school approach is wholly inappropriate for your puppy's proper development, and goes against everything I have written and advised about their well being in

"FIONA, ARE YOU SURE THIS IS THE RIGHT DOG CLUB?"

this book. If you take the 'boot camp' route your puppy would have to get used to another new environment, unnecessary stress, separation from you and you would be faced with a huge bill.

You and your puppy need to learn from each other and by understanding your dog's mental and physical requirements, the bonding process is accelerated. The more effort that you put into the training, the greater the rewards will be. If at a later stage you want to improve you and your dog's skills further, there are a variety of disciplines and advanced classes available to you. These include, working trials, competitive obedience, agility or flyball. Alternatively you may use your dog as a PAT dog that visits people in hospital or rest homes where their presence is regarded as therapeutic and calming. Whatever you decide in partnership, the rewards are amazing and the bond between you and your dog is a life changing experience.

Streets & Parks

All dogs, no matter what breed, will require exercise on a daily basis. Regardless of the weather conditions you will have to grin and bear it, and with the appropriate clothing it can still be a very enjoyable walk. Each breed will have different levels of fitness so be careful not to over-exercise a puppy as this can have serious repercussions at a later stage of its development.

Having attended training class from an early age, your puppy should be confident in the presence of other dogs. Remember though, this environment is controlled by the instructor and consequently your confidence will be higher knowing that there is someone there to help and assist you if necessary. Now that you are on your own, the decisions you make directly affect the wellbeing of your puppy. On the first outing I would strongly suggest that you take another person with you (an adult), just to give you that added confidence. Try and avoid a busy park on this first excursion so the puppy can focus on you and not the gang of dogs in the distance. If you have been taught how to recall your puppy at the classes, remain calm, take a deep breath and have a go. You only have to go a few feet and reward with plenty of praise. The sooner you achieve this discipline the more enjoyable the walks will be for both of you. Take some tasty treats or toys and make this outing very special.

Wherever possible avoid using the same parks on a regular basis. This repetition could result in insufficient mental stimulation and in your puppy's mind it could be claimed as an extension of his garden. Try different street walks and when walking along the pavement avoid your dog smelling lamp-posts and hedges. This soon becomes a bad habit which is putting your dog at risk of contracting an illness. By walking the puppy in the middle of the pavement this restricts the chances and allows you to practice your heel walking exercise.

Obviously if during your outings the puppy has a poo, bag it and bin it. Not only is it a legal requirement, it's anti-social and unpleasant if you don't. By being a responsible owner and picking up, this mitigates the argument of the anti-dog lobbyists from pursuing councils to exclude dogs from public parks.

Section 9
Puppy Maturity

The onset of puberty varies from breed to breed, but normally occurs around nine months of age. This difficult period in a puppy's life marks the start of adolescence, and can be identified by changes in your dog's behaviour. This time is distinctly different in male and female dogs and therefore I will deal with each sex separately.

Male Adolescence

As a male dog's testosterone levels rise he will naturally become much more interested in female dogs. There will be a tendency for him to cock his leg whilst urinating and he will be attracted to any passing dogs in his attempts to identify a bitch. This distraction will be indicated by a less obedient response to your commands and a strong desire to approach these dogs at every opportunity. His desire to be more independent will be marked by an urge to wander further from your control, and can manifest itself by a much more aggressive attitude. This attitude is particularly noticeable when in the company of other male dogs and sometimes people whom the dog does not know.

Female Adolescence

Her coming into season around nine months of age marks puberty in bitches, but it can start as early as six months. Hormonal changes make some dogs particularly troublesome and she can display unusual moods. A season lasts three weeks and this is a time when she is particularly susceptible to mating and pregnancy. There are many indicators of a bitch coming into season and they include: naughty behaviour, frequent urination to spread her scent, an enlarged genital

"HEY BABE SORRY I'M LATE, HAD A LITTLE TROUBLE GETTING OUT"

area, bleeding from the vulva, excessive licking and an irresistible desire for male dogs to chase or mount her. This bitch season or 'period', repeats itself every six to nine months throughout her whole life.

Neutering & Castration

Each dog is an individual so you should consider the benefits and sometimes disadvantages of neutering:

Pro Neutering

1. With bitches, spaying reduces the incidence of mammary tumours.

2. Prevents phantom pregnancies, womb infections (pyometra), ovarian tumours and unwanted pregnancies.

3. In male dogs it removes the risk of prostate problems and testicular cancer.

4. Male dogs are less likely to be involved in aggressive and hypersexual behaviour.

5. Preventing the above is likely to increase your dog's life expectancy.

Against Neutering

1. Neutering can affect the growth rate and maturation of your dog.

2. Your dog could gain excessive weight in later life, unless you control his diet.

3. The coat could lose its shine.

A question I am regularly asked is, at what age should the dog be neutered or spayed. This depends on the reasons for the operation. If it is a medical problem, you will be advised accordingly by your vet. If you have no intention of breeding, then the general rule is to wait until the male dog has reached maturity, average, between nine and fifteen months. With a bitch I would allow her to have a season first and make sure that everything is functioning properly. After the season allow three months to pass, and then have her spayed.

This is a subject that can cause heated debates. It is a personal choice and after evaluating all the evidence, the decision is yours to make. One thing is for sure. There are far too many unwanted dogs with no homes. Would it be the right decision to bring even more into the world?